THE
SUCCESS
FORMULA

The Three Elements For Success
(Change + Innovation + Leadership)

Paul Rigby

authorHOUSE®

AuthorHouse™
1663 Liberty Drive
Bloomington, IN 47403
www.authorhouse.com
Phone: 1-800-839-8640

First published by AuthorHouse   02/02/2012

ISBN: 978-1-4678-8305-4 (sc)
ISBN: 978-1-4678-8306-1 (ebk)

Printed in the United States of America

CONTENTS

C + I + L = Success

Change, Innovation, Leadership

"Simply stated, you must want it bad enough to survive the process required to obtain it. It is the force of your personal passion that gives you the force to break down the wall between you and the thing you desire."

—Anonymous

INTRODUCTION

Leaders today need to change, innovate and show more leadership skills than ever before. They need to lead with passion. Passion should be the driving force to enable leaders to make tough decisions and follow these through. Trust me, there are hundreds of tough decisions for the modern day leader to make every working day. The pressure is immense and I doubt it will taper off in the very near future. At the outset I wish to mention that a leader is anyone with a power base, not just the CEO or MD or director. We have leaders at all levels within an organisation. It is important that we start to recognise this. Change and innovation are critical components to enable an organisation to future-proof itself but they are not the responsibility of only one person. Everyone should understand change and innovation but essentially they are the domains of all leaders who must strive to make change and innovation happen.

When delivering hundreds of speaking engagements in over forty countries throughout the world, I have been told time and time again, "I really enjoyed your talk do you have a book?" Well I am pleased to advise, here it is.

This is a collection of a few of my ideas, thoughts and opinions on change, innovation and leadership based on my experience as a professional speaker, facilitator, consultant and as a corporate employee at all levels within an organisation. It is compiled from information I have gleaned over the years and knowledge I have gained throughout my career plus conversing with thought leaders and participants, whom I have had the pleasure to meet whilst delivering my speaking engagements. I have met some truly inspirational people.

The topics are vast in themselves. There are, of course, a plethora of publications on each of these topics. I have chosen to write on change, innovation and leadership because I strongly believe that these are the three elements of business management that will change the future of corporations. They are, perhaps, the most important focus areas for the next 10 years or so. Every leader should have these elements in their KPI matrix and be judged, measured and paid on their progress. Note: I referred to progress not necessarily their success. Why? Because even if they fail, provided leaders have learned from the experience, it will help and enrich them for the future. Change, innovation and leadership quite simply define those who make it and those who don't—companies that will be here tomorrow and those that will not.

What do these elements (change, innovation and leadership) have in common? We need to take action, trust people, empower people, get our hands dirty, keep the pressure on, be motivated, enthused, energetic, passionate, focused and show a relentless determination to make change, innovation and good leadership happen. We must follow them through to the end. If we do not demonstrate most, if not all, of these fundamental and necessary traits I think it is highly unlikely that change, innovation and leadership will be implemented successfully.

Change, Innovation and Leadership are inter-dependent. I believe it is difficult to reinforce one without the other. Change is needed in everything we do. I often ask in speaking engagements if there is anyone in the audience who does not see the need to change. I have yet to receive a serious affirmative answer to that question. Of course we need to change and keep changing. Innovation is a focused change and leadership is needed to implement both change and innovation. It is as simple as that!

Without good leadership, change will struggle to get off the ground. Without change, innovation will not happen because innovation is really a focused change. Without innovation, the future is bleak and organisations will struggle to survive.

In this book (and during my public speaking engagements) I am averse to over-complicating things. I like to KISS (Keep It Simple Stupid) everything as much as possible. There are far too many complicated issues in the world today. It takes a special kind of intelligence to simplify things. One thing I learnt early on in the business world was to keep it simple and make it crystal clear. While simplicity may not necessarily guarantee success, too much complexity will certainly increase the chances of failure.

"We like stories, we like to summarize and
we like to simplify."

—Nassim Nicholas Taleb[1]

To make change, innovation and good leadership
happen all we need to do is find the right people
who take action and are passionate about what they
do. What could be simpler than that, I ask tongue in
cheek?

"Get the right people on the bus; get the
wrong people off the bus; and then get the
right people in the right seats on the bus."

—Jim Collins[2]

People are your most important asset, right? Wrong!
The RIGHT people are your most important asset.
One of the signs of a great leader, as far as I am
concerned, is one who employs these "right assets",
utilises their strengths properly and keeps them
motivated, productive and passionate in what they
do every day. I honestly believe that it is easier to
teach people with passion and the will to want to win,
than it is to try and teach people who are spineless,

energy sucking and need to be told what to do at every turn. Passion *is* everything. A successful change or innovation initiative requires the right people, the right composition of the team, incredible motivation, undying support and ideally everyone in that team should be passionate about what it is they are trying to accomplish. Passionate people tend to be winners.

I am yet to meet a winner who did not have passion in what they were trying to accomplish. Passion also leads to action. Michael Jordan[3], USA basketball superstar summed it up: "With 30 seconds left in the game, some people want to watch, some people want to pass, some people want to shoot the ball. We want the people who want to shoot the ball."

I love the story about the five frogs sitting on a log. Yes it is an old story but it really brings the point home. I am sure you know it: There are five frogs sitting on a log. One decides to jump. How many frogs are now sitting on the log? Most people will immediately say four. The answer is, still five. The frog only decided. There was no action. We need more action in business today.

One of my all time favourite quotes is from Sara Henderson[4]:

> "Don't wait for a light to appear at the end
> of the tunnel, stride down there and light
> the bloody thing yourself".

This sums it up for me. This is what we need people to do with change, innovation initiatives and in demonstrating our behaviour as leaders.

The issue with businesses today is that we are still stuck with the Pareto Principle scenario of the 80:20 rule where 80% of the work is conducted by 20% of the people. In times of austerity I ask the question; "Why are the 80% still employed?" If we do not address the issue, all we end up doing is annoying the workers and allowing the loafers to benefit. Surely this is not the way to lead a business in the 21st century? I visit many organisations in a calendar year. Time and time again I see people who are quite content to just sit on the log. They sit and wait for the next instruction to come from above. There is no passion except when they want to moan about something. We need to change this behaviour, we need to seek out passionate people and we all need to jump off the log.

Life is short. We spend a lot of our life at work, so why not be happy and passionate about what we do? I recently read a quote that less than 20% of people are happy in their jobs. This is crazy. How can you be passionate if you are not happy? We are all dead a long time, so live life to the full. Be happy. Make the most of every day. Live life like this is your last day on earth and jump off that damn log. Now! This is how we become great leaders. This is how we make change and innovation happen. The formula is really quite simple.

Change + Innovation + Leadership = Success.

This book is based on my knowledge and experience. I hope you will reflect on your working life. Think about your business and then make the changes that need to be made to ensure your organisations' long-term viability. This is a brief overview of the three elements that I believe are so important. This book is purposefully short and to the point. I hope you enjoy reading the three chapters. I hope they give you food for thought, ignite ideas and open up

the passion that lies inside you to make change and innovation happen, to become a better leader and make a difference in everything you do . . . starting NOW.

CHANGE

<u>Personal Change</u>

People seem to enjoy talking and procrastinating in the coffee rooms or corridors instead of taking action. Why is this? Why don't people like change? Is it the fear factor of the unknown or is it that it takes us out of our comfort zone? Probably both. The irony is that I wonder if anyone can really say with confidence that they have a true comfort zone in the business world? I think we are all kidding ourselves. Is there anyone out there who can say with 100% certainty that his or her job is secure tomorrow; or for the next 10 years? Makes you think doesn't it?

A few years ago I had the great privilege of working for a dynamic international company. The people were great, the products were great and the clients were like an extended family. I loved the company I worked for. I worked long hours and was extremely loyal to the company, as were many other employees. I loved my job. We made good profits and hit budget every year and often exceeded Head Office expectations in terms of turnover, net profit and margin percentage. We won awards and we were an innovative, motivated, inspiring, hard working, passionate team. The company culture was awesome. We worked hard and we played hard.

Then one fine April morning (April 1st to be precise, talk about an April fool), I woke to the realisation that everything had changed in my life. I felt as if a bus had hit me. Wham! Absolutely flattened. Get the picture? It was even worse than the intrepid roadrunner in the cartoons. I had been expecting it for a while. I had tried to prepare myself for this momentous event. I had seen most of my colleagues go through it. I was the person tasked with handing them their redundancy papers and discussing the contents with each of them, so it was not as if this was something of a surprise. It had taken a year of planning to get here. I was part of the last group of employees to go. So there really had been plenty of time to prepare. Well I did prepare of course. But the final day came and went and the new morning greeted me with the reality of the situation. Welcome to the real world of hard knocks!

I remember telling myself that I would be ok. I had prepared well for this day. I was a motivated guy. I would make things happen. I was confident in my ability. I was energetic, passionate and a go-getter. (I still am by the way). What happened in reality is that I found myself stuck on the log. I was frozen by fear. I could not jump and I did not want to jump. What if there were things that would eat me in the murky water below? By the way, this is often what happens to people in change situations.

We are emotional beings and need to go through a process of transformation. We need to let go of the past, define what is over and what is not and identify what we are losing and what we might gain. Then we need to normalise, understand where we are and build coalitions. From here we need to reassure ourselves that all is not lost. There is a positive outcome and a bright future. This process takes time. We are all wired differently. Some people get through this transformation faster than others and some people just battle with the whole process.

Fear

I suppose I am lucky. I generally get through these things fairly quickly. I made a decision on April 1 (towards the afternoon I must admit) that I was not going to sit on the log for long. It was time to jump. So I did. I leapt as high and as far as I could. Of course I was still thinking about what was in the murky waters below. I would be a fool and a liar if I denied that. Often fear and a sense of urgency is what drives us. I remember reading a great line in the book *Who Moved My Cheese*?[5] It has stuck with me ever since. It is a simple one liner but has had a profound effect on me.

> "What would you do if you weren't afraid?"[6]

Well, that quote certainly drove me and still does today. I firmly believe that this quote is a question we should ask ourselves every time we have doubts about change, innovation and how we lead. We should do whatever it is we think we should do. Just take action and make it happen. If you are not making a difference it is almost certainly because you are afraid. It is difficult to embrace change, no matter how brightly you paint the picture, if you are frozen in fear. Action conquers fear. Do not get to the end of your life and look back and think, "I wish I had taken more action." Do it now!

> "Fear only sticks around if you hang on to it. It's very interesting. I think of fear as a very boring, very ungracious guest, who will stick around only as long as I entertain him. The best thing to do with fear is to let it go. If you laugh at your fears, then they just disappear. The only way I've ever been able to get rid of fear is to laugh it away.
>
> I realised that two things can't occupy the same space at the same time, and, if I take the space that fear previously occupied and fill it with positive intention and specific goal-orientated action, the fear can no longer occupy that space.
>
> I realised that there are two paths you can take in life. One is seeing life as a series of problems, fears, and failures. The other is seeing life as experiences, opportunities, and adventures. It is exactly the same life.

It's just that the perspective is different. You can either walk path A or path B. The choice is always yours."

-Thea Alexander[7]

An important thing to consider about change is that people will only change once they are comfortable with what they are being asked to change. What do I mean by "being comfortable?" They understand it and can clearly see the benefit. It has been said many times before but it is an important point, worth mentioning here. Change must come from the heart. Once again, passion is key.

Perhaps, as mentioned earlier before an effective change can take place people need to make a transition. They need to go through the emotional side of change. In other words, they need to let go of the old way of doing things, be allowed to reflect and then to be given time to contemplate the way things will be from now on. Transitions are either times of opportunity or times of vulnerability or both. Often people need to contemplate the effect the change might have on them and their colleagues. It is very important to allow people to come to terms with these emotional issues. We often talk about change as if it is a company phenomenon but there is an important part of change that concerns personal change. It needs serious attention because after all, what are we changing? We are changing people's habits and behaviours, nothing more—nothing less.

A good leader will recognise this and allow time for the transition. I must stress that everyone handles these situations differently. I often consult with the H.R. department on such issues to seek advice. I am a firm believer that H.R. has a strategic function. An excellent H.R. manager is a huge benefit to any organisation. Leaders need to make better use of H.R. during times of change and transition. If any H.R. leaders are reading this, please ensure that you understand change and all of its elements.

If you can get people to jump off the log and move to new pastures as soon as possible this is first prize. However, be careful not to push too hard in these situations. It must be stressed that one needs to get certain things out of ones system and in some cases this may be termed "removing the obstacles that prevent change". What often holds people back from moving forward is not necessarily a lack of motivation. It is often the obstacles that are standing in the way. However, without allowing people time to evaluate the situation and to reflect on it true urgency can ever happen and consequently, true change may never materialise. It is important in organisational change to ensure that personal change is considered too.

Take Action

A client once said to me, well actually more than once, that he liked doing business with me because I always came back with a quick reply. It was either yes, or no. He liked that because he knew where he stood and could then act on the answer given, rather than wait for meetings and committees to decide, more delays and procrastination and finally an answer that he may not have liked anyway. Even a negative answer was ok because he knew what action to take next.

The thing is that we all jump off the log at one time or another. What we need to do is jump sooner rather than later or opportunities will go begging. The same applies to change and innovation. Yes, think about the issue or opportunity carefully, but do not procrastinate about it too long.

It is not that people do not like change. That is a myth. People do not mind change, they do mind being changed. So as leaders, if we can nurture and convince people to change, they will change if there is a compelling reason to do so, that is if they are convinced and feel comfortable with the change that is being proposed. Change is in the very fabric of our DNA. Just look at how often we change jobs. Most of the time that is a voluntary decision. Most of us volunteer to have children. Well I cannot think of a bigger natural life-changing event than that. We move house, move from city-to-city, country-to-country etc. all are generally self-imposed changes. So who says we do not like change? We handle it and generally we do pretty well. I think there is too much negativity centred on the topic of change. If left to their own devices, people generally just get on with it. So why don't we do the same in our business lives as we do in our personal lives?

Develop Urgency

I often use the analogy of the motorcar stuck in the mud, accelerating, with its wheels spinning but making zero progress. This is what often happens in the corporate world. There is a lot of activity but little productivity. The wheels just spin and spin and spin and eventually either they lose their tread or the engine burns out. Quite simply, in order to change, action is needed. Why is this so difficult to understand? We often spend a great deal of our day being active when being productive is what we are being paid for. Allow me to explain.

A long time ago in a far away land I was a newly married young man. I was on my honeymoon. We went to the Hwangwe National Park in Zimbabwe, near the Victoria Falls. We were driving in the park on dirt roads in a small Mazda 323 sedan motorcar. All of a sudden, as often happens in Southern Africa, it began to rain heavily. We were doing OK until suddenly, we hit thick mud and were stuck. With a small two-wheel drive sedan, we quickly sunk into the mud and the wheels spun and spun and spun as we tried desperately to get out of a precarious situation.

No matter how hard I tried to free us from the mud, we just ended sinking deeper into the mud. As we had not seen any wildlife for at least half an hour, I decided to impress my new bride, jumped out of the car and attempted to push the car out of the mud while she did her best to hit the accelerator. Well, nothing happened apart from the fact I managed to get covered in mud from head to toe. There was certainly a lot of activity but very little productivity. All I can say is that at that stage, if you had been there, it was definitely not the right time to inform me about your observations on activity versus productivity.

I found a large branch at the side of the road and tried to use it to lever the car out of the mud. Still no productivity, but a serious amount of activity I must add! After what seemed like hours (but was probably a few minutes) little progress was made until there was an almighty roar. It seemed to come from an anthill about 10 metres away. If anyone has had the privilege to hear a fully-grown male lion roar, you will appreciate the sound I am describing and what it "feels" like. Yes, that is not a misprint, the sound feels like something you have never felt before or can even remotely imagine. It is strange what flies through your mind in situations such as these. My first thought (and

I can clearly recollect it even today) was that this was not a movie set. This was the real thing. This was not Clint Eastwood asking me if "I felt lucky?" (Remember that famous scene in the Dirty Harry movies?) I was certainly not in the mood to answer that sort of question, trust me. My rib cage nearly shattered and my chest nearly blew apart with the resonating sound waves emitting from that one tonne lion that I couldn't even see.

Suffice to say that all of a sudden I developed an incredible sense of urgency. In one simple, coordinated and elegant movement I pushed the car out of the mud and climbed in through the passenger window whilst it was moving at speed. It was pure poetry in motion. That move would make a professional stuntman look like a real amateur. I was sure the lion was about a metre behind me but my now ex-wife will beg to differ. It was probably miles away and weighed in reality no more than 150 kilograms at most. Well it sounded a lot closer to me. In my mind it was absolutely huge and I will stick with my version of the story thank you very much. At least we were out of the mud and moving again.

So what is the moral of the story? Watch Dirty Harry movies! No. Seriously, you need productivity not just activity. We are paid to be productive, so make sure that every day, if you want things to happen and change for the better, you are more productive. Activity is easy but it does not always lead to results. Often urgency is the catalyst for change and productivity. It is difficult to change without a sense of urgency—that determination to make something happen NOW. That lion's roar certainly increased my sense of urgency and look what was accomplished. I am not necessarily advocating using the burning platform technique because that instils fear. Just get more people to be urgent every day and watch the incredible results that follow. Do not always strive for perfection on the first attempt, just get things moving and generate momentum.

> "First you jump off the cliff and you build
> your wings on the way down."
>
> Ray Bradbury[8]

Urgency is a must for every organisation in today's ever-changing business environment. Organisations must operate with urgency every day. It is helpful to start with the easy issues that are quick to change to promote the urgency that is needed. It will soon become contagious. When people are thinking and behaving with urgency they believe that action on critical issues is needed now. They do not waste time by engaging in irrelevant activities. They just get on with it. When the rules of the game suddenly change is it so easy to be left behind. So do not allow complacency, do not accept the status quo. It is an easy habit to fall into without even realising it.

> "Never accept or be too comfortable with the status quo, because the companies that get into trouble are historically the ones that aren't able to adapt to change and respond quickly enough."
>
> —Tony Hsieh[9]

Change Is A Team Sport

> "If everyone is moving forward together, then success takes care of itself."
>
> —Henry Ford[10]

Life deals us different decks of cards, so to speak, with many challenges and opportunities. How one reacts to these challenges and opportunities determines the winners from the losers. It goes without saying that change requires winners. Change is difficult, change is challenging and change is even harder to implement alone. If I have learnt something from all of the changes that I have made in my life, it is that change is definitely a "team sport". All the successful changes that I have made in my personal life as well as in my career have been successful due to the team involved. However, if you want to change, you have to have a strong leader—an identifiable person at the top, where change begins in a highly visible way. Let's call the person the change champion.

I can recall a change initiative I once tried to implement that was a total failure. I wanted to change a system that would make the company more efficient. However, in my enthusiasm and determination to get the job done, I forgot to bring people along with me. This wasn't due to arrogance or trying to score points with the boss, it was solely as a result of failing to appoint a guiding coalition and to obtain their buy-in and support, which was absolutely necessary for the change initiative to work. Because of this, the people that I needed to be on my side didn't understand what I was doing and didn't have the same passion to implement the task at hand as I did. I always think whether you succeed or fail you should always learn something from your success or failure and take it forward with you, which I have certainly done. Change is a team sport and the more people you can get on board the change bandwagon the easier it will be to make it stick and be part of "the way we do things around here". So what I did in this instance was to take what I call a "health check" on change. I went back to ensure that everyone had a high sense of urgency. I then formed the change team and we made great progress from there on in. If only I had done that in the first place I would have saved a lot of time and effort.

> "Masters often ask for support in many forms. There is no such thing as a self-made man. You will reach your goals only with the help of others."

> —George Shinn[11]

Get A Quick Win

My pet hate is business meetings. Allow me to be a little more specific. I have a serious dislike for meetings without purpose, structure and discipline with follow up. I often talk about meetings when delivering a speaking engagement. It is a topic everyone can relate to easily. Time and again I am told by people that the majority of meetings they attend are a waste of time, reach no conclusion, take too long, are attended by too many people, the wrong people, there are no actions between meetings, meetings start late and run over time, people spend all of the meeting on their smartphone or on their computer doing email or surfing the net. Minutes or notes are published weeks after the meetings take place, and so it goes on and on and on.

If there is one quick change an organisation can make, and in doing so become more efficient and effective plus have a short term win to demonstrate the effectiveness of change, it can do something positive about the meetings it holds. Why don't leaders take action on this important and often time consuming and productivity wasting activity? Quite simply, taking action regarding the above, is easy to implement and fairly easy to get buy-in for. As they say at Nike, "just do it". Just jump off the preverbal log and take action. Often I mention this to leaders and delegates I meet at workshops and speaking engagements and the response is nearly always the same . . . this is the way we do things around here, this is our culture. Well, my answer to that is . . . your culture stinks. Change it!

If you run a good meeting that is effective, starts on time and finishes on time, has structure and engages people, the attendees will wonder (with genuine regret) why the meeting was so short. Change. Aim to do this at the next meeting you chair. Make it stick.

One Step At A Time

I regularly set action plans with the teams I am consulting with, only to return a few months later to find things are just the same, no action has taken place and thus no change. Well, not in every organisation. Those that have a high sense of urgency certainly make great progress. When I ask why no action was taken, I get people looking down at the table like scorned school children without a proper answer. Of course I hear feeble excuses. After I had left, everyone just went back to doing what he or she had always done. I just do not get it. Some of these people spent two solid days discussing change and telling me how they would change only to put their notes in drawer thirteen never to be looked at again. You will never find new solutions if you keep looking at the same things in the same way. The reason for this is simple. There is no sense of urgency and no passion. People talk the talk but do not really walk the walk. Change takes time and effort but if we take one step at a time and make small incremental changes we will get to where we want to be. As Chip and Dan Heath mention in their book *Switch,*[12] aim to achieve your goal by looking at inch pebbles rather than aiming for milestones. Thanks Chip and Dan for that. Great analogy. I use it often. The steps we take do not have to be large steps but it is critical that we keep moving forward. Long-term success is comprised of a series of short-term successes and continuous momentum.

> "The man who moves a mountain begins by carrying away small stones."
>
> —William Faulkner[13]

Urgency & Passion

Change is also a great opportunity for learning. The issue is that most leaders do not change until the cost of not changing becomes greater than the cost of changing. I ask all leaders (please note that we are all leaders to some extent, I am not just referring to the senior executive team here) to get off the log and make it (whatever *it* is) happen NOW.

Soon is not as good as NOW.

Here is a story that illustrates urgency, passion and to look at things differently, through a different lens: In March 1989, a hairdresser, Phillip McCrory, was shocked to learn about the huge *Exxon Valdez* oil spill off the coast of Canada. He was watching the news where rescue workers were trying desperately to clean the oil off the otters' fur. Then he had one of those bright spot moments. "If oil stuck to fur would it stick to human hair?" He collected hair from his salon and tested it with oil in a plastic swimming pool by stuffing the hair into a pair of pantyhose stockings and created a ring. He then poured motor oil into the centre of the ring of hair and pantyhose. He was right.

The oil somehow clung to the hair and the water was cleared of the horrible black mess.

The oil clung to the hair in the pantyhose. The pantyhose could be wrung out and placed back in the water to absorb more of the oil. McCrory rushed off to a science laboratory to test his findings further and patented his idea. It was found to work extremely effectively and at a fraction of the cost of the method that was previously employed. McCrory built a business on this and you may be amazed to know that hair helped clean up the mess of the 2010 Mexican Gulf oil spill.

I do not mean to belabour the point but urgency is the catalyst for most changes. Get the urgency up in your organisation, starting NOW.

OK, enough on change and transitions. We can write books on the subject and people have already done so. So let's move onto innovation.

INNOVATION

What Is Innovation?

So what is innovation? I have often heard people answer this question by assuming it is the bright idea. Well yes it is and much, much more. The bright idea is only the beginning. But then what?

I have been talking about, studying and implementing innovation for a long time. Innovation is different things to different people. I think it all depends on where you sit within the organisation. I must confess that most of my thoughts and ideas on innovation are strongly influenced by Vijay Govindarajan[14] and Chris Trimble[15] whom I have the extreme pleasure to know and work with. So if there is a slight bias here, you know where it comes from. I do not apologise for this because I believe that I am privileged to have such a great opportunity to be involved, whenever I can, with two humble and esteemed leaders in their field.

The term **innovation** derives from the Latin word *innovatus*, which is the noun form of *innovare* "to renew or change". Although the term is broadly used, innovation generally refers to the creation of better or more effective <u>products</u>, <u>processes</u>, <u>technologies</u>, or <u>ideas</u> that affect organisations, <u>markets</u>, <u>governments</u> and <u>society</u>.

For our definition of innovation and one I learnt from Vijay and Chris, we refer to an innovative initiative as "any project that is new or has an uncertain outcome".[16]

Innovation is not just about new products and services and it does not always entail huge leaps and strides. As with change, gradual step-by-step innovation is innovation too. Gradual innovation is often more important than radical innovation. It will lead to an innovation culture that allows a steady stream of smaller incremental innovations. So please do not think innovation is all about radical ideas and is only about radical innovation. I always stress this point when delivering speaking engagements and facilitating workshops. Participants from around the world often think is has to be something big and audacious. It does not. For example a clerk in the finance department might discover a financial tool that saves costs that translates into price innovation and might lead to the development of a new product in future.

In reality, innovation does not require extensive change. It requires *targeted change*. Innovation *is* the toughest kind of change.

In summary innovation is strategy. To distil this and to clarify it further, innovation is probably the most important part of strategy. In addition, a business needs more than a good strategy. It needs to implement that strategy.

In one of his blogs, Vijay has a fantastic paragraph, quoted below, that brilliantly explains his stance on executing innovation. I mentioned that I like simple and clear communication. Well you do not get any simpler and clearer than this.

> "We liken innovation to an ascent of Mount Rainier. Most climbers focus their energy and enthusiasm on attaining the summit, leaving very few resources for the less glamorous and

more dangerous part of the expedition—the descent. Similarly, companies devote their energies only to reaching the innovation summit—that is, identifying, developing, and committing to a brilliant idea. "Getting to the summit can seem like fulfilment of a dream, but it is not enough. After the summit comes the other side of innovation—the challenges beyond the idea. Execution. Like Rainier, it is the other side of the adventure that is actually more difficult." In short: There is too much emphasis on ideas, not nearly enough on execution."[17]

The Bright Idea!

I hope that you work for a company that has come to realise that without innovation it will die. If you are to be successful in innovation you need to build a new structure for creating successful innovation initiatives. Where does this all start? With creativity! Without creativity there is no innovation.

The bright idea, the creativity is the start of innovation. To get a bright idea is an art unto itself. Organisations spend a lot of time, effort and money creating good ideas. The problem is that they do not spend enough time in implementing these ideas.

Not everyone has bright ideas; or do they? I have found that any idea is a good idea no matter how silly it may seem at the time. Some of my brightest ideas occurred whilst I sat at a table with people brainstorming and "shooting the breeze". They had said something that ignited something else in the far reaches of my mind. I am a pretty hyperactive guy. I find it hard to sit still for any length of time but when the bight idea "lights up" that is when I go into overdrive. How will we market it? What will it cost? How will we communicate it to staff, to clients, to stakeholders? What will the brochure look like? Who will buy it and use it? Is there a market for it? My mind does not follow a set pattern, I just go on a route march in all different directions and all at once.

A lady who used to work with me told me that she disliked it when I travelled because she said that was when I was most dangerous. The team would sit in the office and knew exactly when the plane had landed because the emails would come in at a rapid rate of knots. All sorts of ideas with all sorts of actions I wanted people to take and they had to be completed by the time I returned.

The poor team, they must be pleased to be rid of me now. Well these emails stemmed from ideas generated in the boardroom or over the meeting table somewhere—they often involved change and innovation. I am an avid reader of business books and journals. This is where I often get my inspiration. After reading something that has stimulated my brain, I then try to implement the ideas. I attempt to distil the ideas and focus on a few that I think will make an impact on the business. These bright ideas are the start of the innovation process. The ideas are what I call the sexy part of innovation that everyone wants to be a part of. I am not for one moment saying that these are easy to think of but this is the area that gets the most attention and praise up front. This is the glamour side of innovation, let's be honest. The problem that most of us tend to ignore is that now the hard graft starts.

Probably one of the most innovative ideas I have ever had was to think that mobile phones would be "the next big thing". I heard about mobile phones whilst listening to a radio talk show on my way to work one morning. Mobile phones were not mainstream products in those days. This was pre the Nokia 2010 and Motorola 6200. Remember those handsets?

I convinced my boss to form a separate department (this was the key) and look into mobile phones and how they could compliment the business we were in (which was photocopying and printing). The rest as they say is history. This was an innovative idea that made the company millions (sadly not me) and started with a discussion on a radio talk show, that lead to a discussion in the board room and the belief in me by my mentor at work, to empower me and allow me to take it forward.

I must add that I made the biggest faux pas of my business life not too long after the launch of mobile telephony, when I made a bold statement at the same boardroom table. I said boldly that "pay-as-go" would not work. Today 80% of all mobile connections are "pay-as-you-go". Well it just goes to show that I am human after all.

Why do I bother telling you these stories? To be innovative you must be prepared to make mistakes but you also need someone to back you and believe in you and support you when needed. If you are not innovative as a company, you will surely die because success requires innovation, it does not come from optimising known techniques. The way I see it, innovation is change. It is a focused change. Innovation is more difficult to implement than change because it deals with something new that is uncertain.

Innovation Requires Action

Innovation is a two-part challenge. Initially, you need the breakthrough idea. Then, you have to execute it. Unfortunately, it is the latter part that is usually underappreciated or overlooked as we have mentioned already.

> "We should be taught not to wait for inspiration to start a thing. Action always generates inspiration. Inspiration seldom generates action"
>
> —Frank Tibolt[18]

Innovation and change are the drivers for enhanced efficiency, improved competitiveness and increased profitability. The "best run" organisations are fine-tuned to weed out activities that interfere with productivity or efficiency. This is what makes them great. Great organisations also recognise that they need to create the future. If, however, you maintain an out-dated, innovation-averse work environment then people will stop coming forward with new ideas. This will be a disaster because employees have thousands of ideas that you need to reap and grow and fine tune. Toyota apparently claims that every year 70% of its employees provide ideas and suggestions, many of which are implemented. The problem most great organisations face, however, is that the same great ideas that are needed to create the future also require new activities. These great ideas can interfere with productivity and efficiency. This is the toughest kind of change but if you get this right you create an agile organisation that is better equipped to succeed in the future.

Change is not always uncertain and it is not always new. We may change a system and the result is fairly certain in that it will allow us to be more productive or more efficient. It also does not always involve starting from scratch. We may simply modify or improve something.

Tomorrow's Business Today

It has been quoted by many business leaders and authors in the academic world that 70% of change efforts fail. One of the reasons for this failure, that is seldom mentioned or discussed, is that organisations do not address uncertain outcomes that change initiatives are often faced with. Is this perhaps because of fear? Innovation is probably the one business objective that we cannot predict where it will end up. I think the best way of looking at innovation is to look at where it will lead us, rather than as a set goal with a finite end result. It is probably because of this unknown factor that fear creeps in and thus prohibits ideas and the motivation to innovate on a broader scale. Remember the quote earlier; "What would you do if you weren't afraid?" Too often leaders talk the talk about innovation but fail to walk the walk. They lack confidence in the innovation decisions. Innovation requires leaders and for that matter, everyone else to be courageous, bold and focused about what they wish to accomplish. Failing this, innovation will surely die and the organisation with it.

The issue for business leaders today is how to sustain today's competitive advantage when it is often in direct conflict with what we need to do to create tomorrow's competitive advantage. It is not enough to simply execute today's practices tomorrow; we must begin to execute tomorrow's practices today.

> "In general, we are good at executing today's business tomorrow; We are not good at executing tomorrow's business today".[19]

> -Vijay Govindarajan

Business is dynamic; situations constantly change, so generalisations based on the past often do not apply to the present. Implementing a change effort means doing work in new ways. Even when the expected results of such a change are well understood and senior leadership has massive confidence in the outcomes of the change, there will still be considerable pushback by the forces of daily operations or the performance engine, that is, the engine that pays the bills today.

What happens in reality is that known and existing routines take priority to the unknown and new routines. This alone makes it difficult to implement change even when those changes have the support of executive leadership.

Due to the way we lead, manage and focus our efforts on short-term wins, when the work is new and the outcome is uncertain, one thing is certain; these projects get the least of our attention and effort when they compete with our need to accomplish our daily operations.

The fact is that most management time and attention is focused on managing the present. We must maintain our competitive position today if we are to have the resources to invest in the future. The problem as far as innovation is concerned is that far too many leadership teams put all their eggs in today's basket at the expense of tomorrow.

In looking at future practices, uncertainty poses an even bigger challenge. How do we invest anything in something we have not done before, or something that we do not even know the outcome of?

A New Approach Is Needed

Because of these unknowns, companies often do not commit 100% to innovation. The problem most organisations face when considering innovation initiatives, is they apply the same execution process to both the known and new routines. In other words the planning and repeatability process we employ in the normal course of business will not necessarily apply to innovation initiatives. A totally new approach is needed. Successful innovation initiatives usually employ a totally new approach to the implementation process.

I was once asked to head up a new department. This department would do something different to the existing business and had an uncertain outcome. The task was to form a software department. At the time the company only sold hardware products. This meant changing everything from hiring new staff, to setting new basic salaries and compensation plans, to re-organising the ordering system and warehouse, to using new sales methodologies to existing clients and probably most important of all, to finding new clients we had never bothered to entertain before.

These were just a few of the myriad of challenges and changes we were faced with.

I distinctly remember one of the first obstacles we found in our path was the warehouse team. They were used to moving boxes. The system required everything to pass through the warehouse for invoicing purposes. At the time software was less than 0.01% of the total business. As you can imagine the warehouse team did not pay software much attention. In the big picture, to them, it was a headache they didn't need, especially at month end when 80% of the orders had to move out the door. It is worth noting that on-line streaming of software had started to take off in a big way at this time due to expanded capacity of the Internet. If you did not allow clients to download software on-line, you were just not in the game.

One would think that to provide software to a client was a simple task. Well not in that business at that particular time. We had to deal with people who just would not let go of the past. For nearly a year we had to pack a CD in a box and ship it as a hardware product. It wasn't the systems that could not handle the process because these were adapted and changed fairly quickly, it was getting the warehouse staff to change their mind-set and understand what we were trying to accomplish. They simply kept applying the old system to a new way of working. This was a classic example of applying what is termed "the performance engine" methods to the "innovation engine" process, or the new way of working. It simply does not work. Some things, no matter how hard you try, will give you grey hair. I think we all added a few more grey hairs in that year and some (who will remain anonymous) even looked slightly balder. We did eventually succeed but it was all an uphill struggle. I hate to think of the lost opportunities and what it must have cost us that year in potential lost revenue.

The bright idea to sell the software was easy to arrive at. It was the implementation that was difficult. One thing I have learned from the numerous innovation processes I have been involved with is that you definitely need a dedicated team, hopefully with shared resources and you need support of the senior team too. Innovation is a company wide exercise and must be inculcated into the corporate culture. Not everyone has to be directly responsible for innovation but I strongly believe that everyone (as with change) should understand and support innovation. This is what makes an organisation move from good too great. This is what company survival is based on.

Not only does the organisation attempt to do something that may or may not pay-off—it jeopardizes the engine (on-going operations) that provides the resources needed to stay in business. The issue that organisations typically have to overcome is that on-going operations and innovation teams are usually in conflict. This is a real leadership challenge.

For innovation initiatives to be successful, new work practices must be integrated and refined until they become repeatable as existing work routines. In other words, "until this becomes the way we do things around here". This leads us to the biggest challenge. The issue that most change and innovation initiatives fail to address is all to do with implementation. This is the so-called back-end of innovation. The important part if you like.

The team has to deal with working out how to modify the existing operations model to accommodate new work practices, processes and routines at the same time.

Whose Job Is It Anyway?

The other challenge they are faced with is how to intentionally create tomorrow while they simultaneously try to execute today's business model. Yes, it is tough to be a leader in today's business environment.

So who should contribute to innovation within the organisation? Leaders at all levels within the organisation plus every employee should contribute to innovation, but it is very important to communicate how employees can contribute. Typically, when you see something strange or unfamiliar coming towards you, the natural reaction is to get out of the way. Neither of these actions is suitable for innovation or change. We need to embrace innovation and change and lead by example. We need to ensure that new ideas are implemented for the benefit of the organisations' future by adhering to a disciplined approach and to ensure the organisation becomes more and more agile.

This is real innovation and change. This is what innovation and change are all about.

I think innovation is still in its infancy as a form of management. One of the problems this brings with it is that whilst other functions have clearly defined roles and departments assigned to them such as finance, marketing and sales, innovation often seems to float from department to department and between different levels. Innovation is not a matter for a chosen few it is the responsibility of the entire organisation. This is why it is important that the people at the top actively participate, believe in and role model their intentions and behaviours concerning innovation in a positive way. It will help develop a culture of innovation throughout the entire organisation. At Google for example, everyone innovates.

Successful innovative companies I have worked with typically appoint a Head of Innovation as a senior position. This person has a birds-eye view of all departments and coordinates innovation initiatives for the entire organisation. Often in this day and age one will see a title on a business card, CIO—Chief Innovation Officer. This is definitely a step in the right direction.

Reverse Innovation

Any discussion on innovation would not be complete without a discussion on the dynamics of how innovation itself is changing. Yes, innovation is changing. So just when you thought it was safe to go out there and practise innovation, everything changes. Welcome to the real world!

Welcome to the topic of Reverse Innovation. Reverse innovation is essentially any innovation that is first adopted in the developing world. If large multinationals do not get to grips with this concept they are at serious risk. For most organisations this really is something new and uncertain. The large multinationals know how to compete with their competition today, but todays' competition may very well not be the same competition of tomorrow and herein lies the problem. Reverse innovation is an opportunity for anyone and everyone no matter where they are located to compete. All they need is the passion to go for it.

So the poorer countries and emerging markets are innovating and bringing their innovations to the richer countries of the world. Why is this happening? Because basically the poorer countries cannot afford the products from the richer nations at the price the products are sold in richer countries. It is a crazy assumption to think that products developed in the West or richer countries will sell with slight modifications in the emerging markets. They simply will not, well, not on a large scale anyway. These emerging markets will not simply import from the rich world as soon as they can afford it. This is the old way of thinking about globalisation.

What is needed now is both glocalisation, (invented way back in the 1980's) plus reverse innovation. Glocalisation is a term used to emphasize that the globalisation of a product is more likely to succeed when the product or service is adapted specifically to each locality or culture in which it is marketed. Glocalisation combines the word *globalisation* with localisation.

Glocalisation today and tomorrow is about (among other things) promoting from within. By this I mean it is about appointing a senior leader or CEO who is born and bred in the country in which the organisation is operating and leading the business within that country. However, it is not just about promoting from within a specific country. It is also about moving the people to and investing wisely within that country and in particular, an emerging market too.

It should be noted that where glocalisation has a flaw, is that in the past it treated rich and poor countries alike. This must change however, in order for innovation initiatives to succeed. The success will come when organisations learn how to execute reverse innovation and glocalisation simultaneously. This is a tall order, but one that must be addressed. Organisations already understand and know how to execute glocalisation initiatives. What they now need to understand is how to roll out and implement reverse innovation initiatives.

The days of the ex-patriot leaders being appointed from the rich countries are fading fast. In many cases now, it is about appointing a head of a large multi-national from outside the so-called rich countries. Think about the great rivals Pepsi whose CEO, Indra Nooyi, was born and educated in India and Coca Cola whose CEO, Muhtar Kent, although born in USA is of Turkish decent and has spent a large part of his career in Turkey, Iran, India and Thailand, as high profile examples. An understanding of emerging markets is key.

Reverse innovation is probably one of the most important tools an organisation has in order to capitalise on the huge growth areas of the emerging markets of Asia, Africa, Eastern Europe and Latin America. It should be noted that at the end of 2011 Brazil moved ahead of the UK as the 6th largest economy in the world. Unbelievable when you look back in history and consider that the Portuguese only decided to visit it as an afterthought.

Reverse innovation holds huge opportunities for the developing world because it is difficult for an innovator based in the USA or Germany to truly understand the needs of a person in Brasilia, Beijing, Lusaka or Mexico City.

The issue is all about legacies. We need to selectively forget the past and think of new ways of doing things, to un-learn and re-learn. The legacies are often what hold organisations back. A few notable examples spring to mind. Polaroid is probably one of the more famous.

I worked in the mobile telephony industry when mobile telephones were more of a gadget than a necessity. One of the main benefits of rolling out the network was that there was no legacy system to update. There simply was nothing in place apart from a landline operation. This was true for all of Africa. As a result Africa, well in particular South Africa leap frogged the USA and Europe in its sophistication and products in a very short space of time. I was party to one of the first on-line secure handset transactions involving payment by mobile phone. This was 20 years ago. I notice that this is only now becoming mainstream in the UK. There are many products that have been designed in Africa and other developing regions that have been reverse innovations and many more will come. Watch this space!

Start With A Clean Sheet

A quick tip but an important one on reverse innovation is that one needs to start with a clean sheet. Do not try to incorporate existing products into an emerging market by merely taking out a few parts here and there or making a few cosmetic changes. This just does not work. An excellent example is the Tata motorcar, the *Nano*. Tata started from the bottom up and launched the *Nano* in early 2008 after 4 years of hard work. Ford tried to combat the *Nano* with a cheap version of a car that Ford had designed in the rich world. They tried to get the price down to that of the *Nano* (approximately $2500) by shaving parts off here and there. It was a failure. One of the cost cutting exercises was to take out the electric windows from the rear. Well this backfired horribly because most people who are in the market for a small vehicle in India sit in the back of the vehicle and do their work or make calls whilst a driver takes the best route to get to their destination. If you have ever been to India, you will understand the issue with traffic. I love the place but there is no way I would drive there.

I am following with interest to see how the *Nano* takes off in Europe and other parts of the world. I live on a small island. I can tell you that if the *Nano* were available here, it would sell like hot cakes. The speed limit is 50km/hr. Why people buy fancy German cars here is a mystery to me!

The question I would like to receive the answer for is whether or not Ford, GM, Mercedes, Toyota, Audi, Honda, Nissan and the rest saw the Nano as a threat a few years ago? As I mentioned earlier, new competitors from emerging markets are coming to the fore every day. What is it Alvin Toffler once said in his book *Future Shock*? "The future is not what it used to be."[20]

There are many examples of reverse innovation successes already, from motor manufacturers and medical equipment in India to banks in Bangladesh. In India a $35 Linux based computer was launched in July 2010 with the aim to reduce the cost even further. Prices as low as $10 were branded in the press. Imagine the impact this will have on the education market worldwide. Recently Godrej and Boyce, one of the largest conglomerates in India, launched a robust $65 refrigerator that runs on a battery. This will be a new trend in business. The established players had better beware because they stand to lose more than a lost opportunity, they stand to lose their market share too.

Innovate With Discipline & Learn

All innovation should be managed with discipline with the focus on resolving the unknowns as quickly and inexpensively as possible. It does not matter whether they originate in rich or emerging countries, make sure there is discipline and make sure there is a learning experience.

For me the issue with innovation is that most people talk about the front-end of innovation. Even when I attend conferences and exhibitions on innovation, it always seems to be front-end focused. This is the sexy part, the new ideas etc. Where they should be focusing on is the back end of innovation. This is the difficult part. This is where the rubber hits the road as they say in the USA. This is where the sweat and tears happen, where innovation is implemented. A sale is not a sale until the money is in the bank. Well innovation is not innovation until it has been run as a disciplined experiment and either we have learnt from that experiment or we have implemented the innovative idea or preferably both. Until then it is just an idea.

So the question is:—

Are you managing today or creating for tomorrow?

> "Before Google, when competition was local, generating an innovation would give you an edge for a very long time.
>
> Today, your competitors will quickly duplicate your innovation, taking away your advantage. To thrive in this business environment, you must constantly disrupt the status quo. Incorporate **innovation** and **change** into how you conduct business every day".

—Seth Godin[21]

LEADERSHIP

<u>Leadership Or Management?</u>

Change, innovation and leadership, as mentioned before, are the three important competencies that will make, break or future-proof an organisation (if done well) for the challenges that lie ahead. After all, good leaders should be thinking about tomorrow and looking for long term, not just short-term results. The short-term results are yesterday's long-term strategies. (Well at least they should be). We need to spend more time focusing on the long-term initiatives. This is why I am adamant that you should pursue your passion and interests and maximise your strengths in order to be successful. If you focus on and play to your strengths, you will have a higher chance of succeeding in whatever you choose to do. Hopefully you are a leader in an organisation that you are passionate about and want to be a part of for years to come. (If not perhaps it is time to move on).

The issue is that, typically, leaders are paid to focus on the short term. They are driven by stock prices and shareholder value. To some extent, to the detriment of the very organisations they are paid to represent, because some unscrupulous leaders "tweak" short-term results to ensure that they receive benefits from their compensation plans. But that is another story. Let us focus on positive leadership, what makes a good leader and how change, innovation and solid leadership provide the platform for success.

Today's companies require more leadership than management. But is there a difference? It is a commonly held belief that managers plan, organize and control. Leaders inspire, set the vision and motivate. Managers often get lost in detail whereas leaders provide the vision. Management is all about coping with complexity. Leadership is all about coping with change. Many contend that managers and leaders provide two different functions. However, consider this: managers lead and leaders manage.

I believe that the two <u>are</u> different. In todays organisations you must have the right balance of managers and leaders. This balance will depend on your industry and outside influences. One thing I know is that in this turbulent business environment, more leaders are needed than ever before. But leadership without management is a disaster.

Are Leaders Born Or Made?

The other myth about leadership is that good leaders are born not made. I firmly believe that leadership is built on action, passion, hard work and the ability to learn—through self-education and deliberate practice. Leaders are undoubtedly made. If people have the right attitude, you can teach them the necessary skills.

What is leadership? The leader is the person who looks at the big picture, thinks, makes his/her mind up and says "team we are going east." A good leader has an innate ability to quickly sum up the situation and know where the wind is blowing. As the famous ice hockey player Wayne Gretsky[22] was quoted as saying when asked how he was such prolific goal scorer: "I go where the puck is, not where it has been."

Play To Your Strengths

There is no one leadership style that fits all leaders. We are all wired differently, we have different strengths and weaknesses and react to situations differently. Good leaders play to their strengths and spend more time on their strengths than their weaknesses. It pays to do so. Good leaders understand this and hire people to fill the gaps created by their weaknesses.

I am not interested in accounting. To be honest it is not the most exciting subject I have ever studied. I get bored with it. My balance sheets do not often balance. Hence I cannot technically call them balance sheets. I prefer to be out of my office interacting with people. I have thus always hired excellent accountants whom I can trust and work with. One such person I was lucky enough to work with in a business I took over in Botswana, is Shekar Ranganathan. That was 20 years ago. He has since moved back to India but we are still good friends today and keep in regular contact. I trust him implicitly and know that he is a person of high moral standards. I knew I could leave the financial side of the business to him and empower him to run it. I knew that at the end of every month at least he could balance the books. Now here is the thing. It was actually Shekar who was empowering me when I think back. He would keep a tight reign on anything I wanted to buy and any lunches I put in expense claims for. He is one tough accountant. I don't know if he knows this, but I felt guilty, well more like scared, when I took a client for an extended lunch, because I would have to submit my expense claim to him for signing afterwards. Sometimes I just didn't bother.

How Important Is The Team?

This leads me to the team, in particular, the leadership team. This is vital for the success of the company. If you are to change and innovate you need a strong team with passion, integrity and in whom you can trust. A weak senior leadership team can bring a company down quicker than any opposition. The issues between the top team will spread to their departments and cause ripples throughout the company. Silos will quickly form and the devastation will take ages to fix. Change will never get off the ground and innovation will be but a distant dream.

I worked in a company where the leadership team were constantly at war with one another. We were successful in spite of ourselves. I often wonder just how successful we could have been had we worked as a team. It was a difficult period but a fantastic learning experience and one I will never ever tolerate again.

Teamwork is vitally important if you are to implement effective change and innovation. The whole team must buy into the change or innovation initiative 100% and be seen to support it. 100% means just that. 99% will not suffice. Employees are more astute than we sometimes give them credit for. They will pick up, very quickly, if there is a split in the ranks. The doubters in the organisation will pounce on the weakness and expose it to the detriment of the change or innovation initiative and to the detriment of the organisation.

The leadership team must be a tight unit with each and every member of that team trusting and respecting each other. Being a strong leader and establishing trust is critical. There is a saying, "what goes on tour, stays on tour". I like to adapt this to reflect "what goes on in the boardroom between the senior team stays in the boardroom". Of course not everyone will always agree with one another all of the time but there is nothing more powerful than a senior team that portrays "togetherness". In a healthy conflict or as I sometimes call it, a violent agreement, put all issues on the table and discuss them with objectivity. Conflict, like trust and interdependence is a necessary part of becoming a real team. A team that is really committed is one of the most productive and powerful tools at the organisations disposal.

Never let disagreements become personal, after all, the team is there to benefit the business. In successful organisations it is the excellent behaviour of the leaders that dissipates throughout the organisation. Never forget that behaviour is contagious, good or bad. Have your issues within the confines of the four walls but when you step out into the office show unity and strength. Not only does it show good leadership, earn you respect as an individual, respect as a team, but it makes the staff feel comfortable and confident.

Early in my career we had an operations director who headed up sales and marketing. There was an issue between the two senior heads of department. Everyone knew about it. It was unpleasant and demotivating for all. One day the operations director had had enough of this childish banter between the two. He had heard that the two of them had been calling each other derogatory names behind each other's backs in the open office in front of the staff. He took the bull by the horns, called them into his office, closed the door and told them to address the issues they had with each other face to face or basically they were fired then and there. I admired his direct approach. It worked. They sorted out their differences, both stayed and their relationship improved. Teamwork is a powerful attribute.

Hiring the most talented people doesn't guarantee success unless they come together as a team. Great leaders bring teams together and motivate their team members to change their attitudes from "me" to "we". The best teams have members who each know what to do. Your team members should each be able to explain their daily mission, objectives, vision and strategies. They must understand the urgency of their jobs. This places everyone in the same boat, rowing in the same direction at the same speed. When team members know the factors that determine their success, they are more motivated and have a better sense of direction and motivation.

As a leader you should try to focus on the individuals strengths and to convince people to volunteer their strengths for the benefit of the team. Teams are made up of individuals who each contribute something special. It goes without saying that the best teams consist of members with differing strengths. Keep this in mind and do your best to be an effective coach to each member of the team.

As Tom Coughlin, coach of the New York Giants, once said, "Coaching is making players do what they don't want to do so that they can become what they want to become".[23]

There will be situations where the leadership team just do not bond together. This is reality. As a leader you must take action. You must stand up and be counted. I often go with my gut feeling. A good friend of mine, Ken Harper, whom I have known for many years, we stated doing business together in 1986, would often tell to me if there is even a little doubt, then there is doubt. So if there is an issue get it sorted quickly.

I was asked to head up a company where the five incumbent directors were at loggerheads. The atmosphere in the boardroom was diabolical to say the least. The business was in trouble and needed serious action to fix it. It needed a cohesive team at the top, which it clearly did not possess. Within three months

I completely changed the executive team. Only one of the five directors remained. I took decisive action in order to fix the team, which in turn fixed most of the issues within the business due to the fact that we played to everyone's strengths, trusted each other and worked as one.

Great leaders focus more on their followers than on themselves. Remember too that there is no such thing as an unwilling follower only one who has no compelling reason to join. Passionate leaders inspire and motivate people to achieve aspirational goals for the organisations' benefit.

> "The difference between management and leadership is that management is working on your business and leadership is working on your people."

> —Cy Wakeman[24]

It's All About The People— Listen To Them

Good leaders have a high emotional IQ. They do not necessarily need to be the most intelligent or the most inspirational (although this helps). I once had a discussion with a client in Egypt. We used to call him "the wise old fox". He had sayings and quotes for every occasion. We were discussing intelligence and the fact that so many people obtain MBA's and numerous degrees these days. The conversation moved to experience versus formal education to leadership and in particular to leaders with less formal qualifications than the people who reported to them. During the conversation he came out with a quote something like this, that made perfect sense: "without clever people, leaders cannot hope to succeed, but without good (experienced) leadership, clever people may never realise their full potential". He went on to say that good leaders should always value their people and be humble. They, above all, need to learn the art of listening. Now do you understand why we called him the wise old fox?

Some leaders spend so much time focusing on making the business better that they forget to pay attention to the human and emotional side, to the very people who are helping them run the business.

My mentor when I was a young product manager was Jac Moolman. He was the Managing Director. He was an incredible listener. He paid attention to everything you said and made you feel important no matter what the conversation. After all, it is futile to be innovative if no one will listen. He taught me humility, he taught me (well he certainly tried very hard) manners, he taught me to bond with your team and with people in general and many more things besides. He would walk around the office every day and greet people, talk to them and share things with them. I remember thinking once, "what the hell is an MD doing walking around, isn't he supposed to be doing MD things?" I used to watch him and study him. I am not sure if he was aware of this, but I did. I observed him in meetings with staff, clients, and international suppliers, at parties and even with his family. I once followed him around the building to observe him and watch whom he was talking to. I thought he had favourites (perhaps he did) but I never recognised this. He spoke to the store man, the receptionist, the head of HR, the credit clerk, the delivery driver, the tea lady (yes we used to have an awesome tea lady, her name was Betty, she was the best), the junior salesperson, the sales manager, the janitor, the finance director. He never segregated people. I never once heard him shout at anyone, not even me and trust me, I deserved it more than once. People would do anything for Jac because they trusted him. Why did they trust him? Because he cared and it showed. He listened. He knew every employee by name. He was humble, cool, calm and collected. Quite simply he has a presence about him that no one else I have ever met has.

When I started my own business I tried to emulate Jac. I tried to do what he did. I believe it paid off and still does today. I will never be Jac and he will never be me, we are different but it pays to emulate the good behaviours from people (anybody in fact) when you recognize them. Good leaders role model good behaviours, which is an art unto itself but goes to illustrate my point; good leaders may be born but they can also be taught.

It is important for any leader to have a mentor. If you are not fortunate enough to learn from a mentor whom you really look up to, then it is time to find a coach. Everyone needs to talk to someone.

Empower People

One of the finest attributes of good leaders is that they empower people and let them feel empowered.

People need to feel happy when they come to work. If people are happy, they have a better chance of being successful. By empowering people this will go a long way to their overall happiness and thus effectiveness. Not everyone wants to be the CEO. Most want job satisfaction. Empowerment goes a long way to fulfilling job satisfaction. After all, if you have to make all of the decisions yourself, then you may as well fire the managers.

Effective leadership is a function of influence and influence is a function of power. The best way to help employees make decisions is by allowing them to learn from experience, including failure, because your best judgements are often based on your accumulate experience.

We often think that being successful leads to happiness but the opposite is true. Success does not lead to happiness, happiness leads to success. Numerous studies have confirmed this over the years. If your leaders feel empowered and thus happy, they will produce extraordinary results. Their teams in turn will follow. It will spread throughout the organisation and the culture will soon become a happy and successful one. If you keep holding people back they will more likely seek employment elsewhere. People need to feel loved, they need to feel wanted and they need to be able to make decisions and learn from those decisions.

The problem is that many of the leaders today are from the old school where they cling to their power base. Why do they do this? They simply cannot let go of the old way of doing business and do not want to change. In today's fast moving business environment, there is no place for yesterday's leadership behaviour. The leaders from the old school and in fact all leaders need to un-learn and re-learn in order to maintain their success. If they are not prepared to do this, then it is time to cut the string, let them move on and replace them. This is a hard fact, but simple reality.

Set The Scene—Make Your Mark

One thing about taking over in a new role is that the first meeting sets the scene for the future and sets the tone for those meetings that follow. It demonstrates to the team who you are and what your intentions are.

In a previous life, I had just been promoted to director and called a meeting with the sales team. I was unhappy with the attitude of a few of the members of this particular team. I called a sales meeting (bearing in mind that most were mature adults who had been in sales and senior positions before. The average age of the team at that time was about 40). I informed the team that I wanted to see a few changes and in particular a change in their attitude. Specifically, I wanted them to be more understanding of what other departments did to support them. This particular team had experienced a period of "hell" under the previous sales director so understandably they were not, at that time, in the best of spirits. I informed them that as the sales team they were probably the best team in the company to lift the spirits of the entire staff. What I saw was unacceptable behaviour from most of them in that they displayed an attitude of apathy, discontent and complacency. This attitude rubbed off on the rest of the staff. I cannot stand complacency. There is no room for it in my world. I politely informed the sales team that from Monday morning (the meeting was held on Friday afternoon) if they did not walk into the office with the right attitude and were not happy, they should tender their resignation with immediate effect. I could not make them happy, I informed them. I could demotivate them, I could also motivate them, but happiness comes from inside as does passion. They had the weekend to make themselves happy and to think about the passion issue. Happiness is a close relative of that word I use time and time again, passion. I wanted passion. I understand that perhaps not everyone is as happy and as passionate as I am, but a little improvement would go a long way.

Every morning they should want to come to work, to do their best, to make it happen, to be fulfilled, to be positive. If they were not prepared to do this, I told them, then they should not bother coming into the office on Monday morning. Harsh words perhaps, but I strongly believe that it is better to have one person with passion than forty people who just want to get it done, as the saying goes and I strongly believe this to this day.

Well come Monday morning they stood up to be counted. All arrived on time, I might add that this was a first too, with smiles on their faces and a more positive attitude. I am not sure that they were all genuine smiles but the facade was enough for me and over time this team developed into a formidable sales team who were more open towards the marketing department, the technical department, the finance department, the warehouse team and the administration department. Sales doubled within a year and margins improved significantly too.

Positive & Passionate Leaders Needed

Isn't it crazy that people who love their work often describe themselves as lucky? Yet luck is not a happy accident. Your attitude plays an important role. Luck often follows those who are passionate, optimistic, hardworking, determined, energetic and confident. Senior leaders get to where they are by adhering to these principles; they have strong work ethics. It is no coincidence that luck comes their way. Makes you think, doesn't it!

Leadership, change and innovation should come from the heart. There are simply so many things going on in a day that if the passion to perform these three critical elements does not come from the heart then they will surely suffer and in due course so will the organisation. There is no doubt about this. We are back to that word again, passion.

> "If you try to lead with your heart and hands, but without your head, you'll seem irrational. If you lead with head and hands, but no heart, you'll seem phony.

If you lead with head and heart, but no hands, you'll appear incompetent."

—Douglas Conant[25]

It is difficult to get this right but leaders should gauge their progress with these statements quoted above, in order to be effective.

Leaders Must Un-Learn & Re-Learn

We are still trying to manage tomorrow's issues and opportunities with today's management style, when we really need to manage tomorrow's issue and opportunities with tomorrow's management style. This is where the un-learn and re-learn comes to play. As I have stated already, if leaders are not prepared to accept this and change their ways, it is time to move on. The world is rapidly changing especially from a technological perspective. But not only that, leaders have to consider various social, ecological, innovation changes and whatever else is thrown at them. They also have to deal with different personality styles of generation X, generation Y, plus gender balance and so on. These are just a few of the myriad of challenges that leaders must cope with on a daily basis. If leaders do not have an open mind, they will surely fail. Related to this, it is vital that leaders have an ability and willingness to continue to learn in the work environment whilst performing their daily routines.

Leadership is not about you; it is about them. As a leader your job is to take people from where they are today to where they need to be tomorrow. Leadership is not about the leader. It is about the positive change that a leader can instil while working with others.

How can leaders do this if they are not prepared to change? Change their style, selectively let go of the past, un-learn and re-learn, empower people, do things differently and be prepared to get out of their comfort zones? Leaders today have an enormous number of tasks to contend with, oh and by the way just add these too; continue to make profits and "be green" whilst growing the market and expanding into BRIC countries and emerging markets. Phew!

As a leader it is also your job to develop autonomy and confidence in your people. It is your job to build employee confidence, teach your staff to answer their own questions and allow them to take appropriate action. After all, greater confidence means greater competence. People are not stupid; they will figure things out themselves if you allow them.

Be An Excellent Communicator

A good leader communicates in a clear, unambiguous way, leaving no stone left unturned and ensuring as many people "get-it" as possible. A good leader should set the big-picture direction, communicate it and get out of the way. Of course not everyone will get it. However, if you use different methods of communication to appeal to as many people as possible, then the greater your chances that more people will be on your side and participate in the change or innovation initiative. We all know the more people on board the change and innovation bandwagon the easier it is to make it happen. Good leaders will obtain the buy-in if they are clear in their communication

I often share this story with clients about the typical month end meeting where the CEO bumbles on about things, then the Finance Director bumbles on about spreadsheets full of numbers that few people understand, let alone can clearly see and so the meeting trundles on. The audience grows agitated and no one really pays attention. I ask clients why they persist in holding the meetings and why are the meetings so boring? The response in more cases than not is that the employees want to understand what is happening in the business and specifically asked for these meetings. Well I doubt they asked for forty minutes of boring trash that was hastily thrown together and mumbled through with zero enthusiasm.

I advise that a different approach is considered. Instead of a power point presentation, use flip charts or posters. The audience should see and feel the message you are trying to convey. Words account for 7% of impact in any presentation, vocal component 38% and the visual component a huge 55%. I will repeat that, visual impact 55%. When, for example, the head of finance stands up to deliver the numbers, do not allow him/her to use excel and power point. Do something different. Dare I say, change! Prepare well in advance and get the marketing team or an outside printer to create a few posters that are placed strategically around the room. Use posters that relate specifically to the information that is pertinent and important. If the desired margin percentage that the organisation needs to attain is 25%, then simply put that figure on a colourful poster with a relevant picture in the background. Ask the staff what they think it stands for. Let them think of answers, then reward the correct answer with a bottle of wine, a CD voucher or similar. Trust me they will remember the margin percentage number for a long time to come. Why? People cannot give their full attention to dull information.

This not only allows for interaction and participation in the meeting but by using the posters people get the message, they buy-in. Just take a little time and effort and think out of the preverbal box, do something different and use a different medium to get your point across. It works, it costs very little and more people will buy-in to the message you deliver. Communication is vital. Effective communication is not about buzzwords or acronyms; it is simple, clear and unambiguous.

> "Make everything as simple as possible, but no simpler."

> —Albert Einstein[26]

A quick tip on communication I was taught by a client during one of my speaker engagements; never assume that everyone understands because they don't and communicate often especially in bad times.

We often receive too much of the wrong communication. Too many emails are one form of communication that spring to mind. I like the idea many organisations use of having a "no internal email day". People have to get away from their desks and computers and actually talk to someone else. Oh my goodness me, I hear the generation Y people saying. Yes, I am sorry to announce that I am asking people to talk to other people in the same office instead of using twitter, email, sms, Facebook etc. I mean seriously, how difficult is it to talk to someone?

So how much communication is enough? You cannot have enough. Well, let me clarify that, you cannot have enough of the right communication. The lesson for leaders and in fact everyone is communicate, communicate, communicate, especially when change and innovation are concerned.

When I travel around the world and visit companies, I often ask people; "What is the primary means of communication in your organisation?" The answer inevitably is email. Then I ask them how many have had structured email training. Surprisingly very few answer in the affirmative. This is crazy. This needs to change. My other famous question is to ask them; "Is there is a bcc on the email address box?" Why do we need bcc? It is a cowards way of trying to either cover your @@@@ or to clandestinely stab someone in the back. Ugly! Stop using bcc and confront people face to face and resolve the issue if there is one.

Carefully controlled conflict can be useful at work but back stabbing just leads to serious politicking and, in the end, de-motivated teams. Leaders cannot communicate effectively unless they show respect for others. Using bcc is certainly not in adherence with this school of thought.

Just remember this. It is hard to read emotional feelings on an email. We all have emotions. Emotions are a powerful tool in communication. Furthermore, it takes less energy to have a legitimate confrontation than it does to keep avoiding the issues. If you have an issue with someone, go directly to the source. Talking to someone else often does not resolve the issue. Including others in a bcc is tantamount to disloyalty and gossiping and will do the person who sent the bbc email no favours.

There are exceptions for using bcc of course. That is where you need someone to be aware of the information but they do not need to be involved in the future correspondence. As I have indicated, make sure it is used for the purpose for which it was intended.

Culture Is Everything

A leader's influence is powerful and often sets the culture of the organisation. The actions of the organisation's leaders determine whether its culture fosters change and innovation. I gave an example previously about (Jac Moolman) my mentor. He was a powerful leader in that he had tremendous influence through his integrity and respect. A leader's influence matters far more than any of his or her individual, solitary ideas.

The culture of an organisation is everything. I often sit in the reception of organisations I visit to try and ascertain what their culture is. I like to arrive early for appointments to allow myself time to reflect on this. It is an interesting exercise to sit in a reception and watch how people react to incoming phone calls, to visitors and colleagues. You can glean a tremendous amount of information just sitting in the reception and observing.

A clear indication of the culture is the timing issue. There is nothing more annoying for me (other than meetings without purpose etc.) than a meeting that starts late. I find it disrespectful to the people attending the meeting, to the presenter and to the employees who may be inconvenienced later due to the meeting running over time. It clearly demonstrates the company culture.

I was recently delivering a workshop for a team of senior executives. The start time was 8:30 am. We eventually started at 9:15am. What was hilarious, well I say this tongue in cheek, is that the first topic of conversation was about urgency and how to increase urgency within the organisation. What a brilliant example to start the day with. When I questioned the team about the late start, the answer I received startled me even more than the fact that we started 45 minutes late. It was explained to me that this was the culture. When I questioned this because I could not and still do not understand it, I was told that I simply had to accept it. I find this not only pathetic, but also arrogant and ridiculous. Here we were discussing how to improve things within the organisation with an obvious short-term win staring the executives in the face and they disregarded it with such ease.

Leaders need to act with urgency every day and ensure the culture of the organisation reflects this. Furthermore, they must role model the behaviours themselves as culture often permeates from the top.

> "The thing I have learned at IBM is that culture is everything."

> —Louis V. Gerstner[27]

Learn From Doing

It was mentioned previously that we need more leaders than managers in the fast changing business world. I think one of the main challenges for H.R. and learning and development professionals, is to nurture and train more leaders. Without strong leadership, organisations will surely struggle and are at serious risk of failure. Organisations must train leaders at every level within the organisation. By this I mean develop leaders who will adhere to a culture of accountability and performance, leaders who truly understand the importance of change and innovation and many other pertinent competencies besides.

> "The wind and the waves are always on the side of the ablest navigators."
>
> —Edward Gibbon[28]

We must allow potential leaders and incumbent leaders to learn from doing rather than _always_ taking them away to learn. Of course we need to train them but we also need to allow them to learn whilst implementing on a daily basis. Leadership development is all about action.

I believe it is an indisputable fact that without proper leadership most good ideas and strategies will fail.

> "Good business leaders create a vision, articulate the vision, passionately own the vision, and relentlessly drive it to completion."
>
> —Jack Welch[29]

CONCLUSION

So, here is the thing . . . you do not need to change or innovate in order to survive? Survival is not mandatory but neither is change or innovation. It strikes me however, that the successful companies of tomorrow will be those that do change and do innovate and have leaders who do lead by example, role model their behaviours and allow their appointed teams to make decisions. They focus on change and innovation as if their lives depend on it. They ensure change and innovation are implicit in the culture of the organisations they lead. (Note however, that when a team at the top wishes to change the organisational culture, it should also change its own culture). They continually strive to improve themselves by un-learning and re-learning. Successful execution of a strategy requires more than just a great leader; it requires a great team.

Good leaders understand this and act as mentors for their team and encourage the "we" approach to business.

I am also firmly of the belief that in order to change, innovate and lead effectively requires a commitment; not just a commitment but a commitment to a commitment. I often ask people to make a commitment. Once we have agreed to the commitment, I ask them to write it down on a piece of paper and sign it. They look at me as if I have just dropped in from Mars. My premise is that it is easy to commit these days but making a commitment to a commitment is something more powerful. By writing this down on paper and signing it, is like a bond, it is stronger than your word. It really is a commitment because it is staring you in the face and you cannot avoid it. You cannot deny it later. It also makes you think long and hard about what it is you are actually committing to. Try it the next time you ask someone for a commitment to do something; be they work colleagues, your spouse, even your children and watch their reaction.

While people may comply with what we want, they commit to what they really want. Commitment makes all the difference. I love commitment.

Leadership, change and innovation also evolve around trust. A small word but a powerful thing is trust, with huge meaning and implications. If you do not trust the team you are working with there will be little success in whatever you are trying to accomplish.

Do not forget that change should never be implemented just for the sake of changing. It should be well thought out and planned, as should innovation.

You may have noticed that I am someone who believes in action. I mentioned the analogy about the five frogs. Action makes everything happen, obviously. Leaders must take action.

> "Success isn't a result of spontaneous combustion. You must set yourself on fire."

> -Arnold Glascow[30]

This book is an overview of the business elements I am passionate about. Of course they should be covered in much more depth. That is fine; one can read further in many books available on the market. I have given an overview, which I hope will make you think and leave you wanting more. I believe these elements are extremely important and will have a massive impact on how organisations will progress. I wrote this book in order to condense my thoughts for a quick and easy read. I hope it has made interesting reading but most of all I hope it ignites passion for ideas and action that you will take into the business world starting NOW.

I must end the book with the "P" word. Quite simply, passion is the gasoline for success.

> "Making passion contagious requires translating your emotion, your vision and your commitment into a language (others) understand and want to hear."

> -Frank Luntz[31]

BIBLIOGRAPHY/ REFERENCES

Introduction

1. Taleb, Nassim Nicholas. *The Black Swan: The Impact of the Highly Improbable.* 2007. London: Penguin Books, 2008. Print.

2. Collins, Jim. *Good to Great: Why Some Companies Make the Leap . . . And Others Don't.* London: Random House, 2001. Print.

3. Jordan, Michael Jeffrey. Six Time NBA basketball champion and many more accolades besides.

4. Henderson, Sara. *From Strength to Strength: An Autobiography.* 1993. Australia, Sydney: Pan MacMillan, 1996. Print.

Change

5. Johnson, Spencer. *Who Moved My Cheese: An Amazing Way to Deal with Change in Your Work and in Your Life*. Reading: Vermillion-Random House, 1998. Print.

6. Op Cit ii P100

7. Alexander, Thea. *2150 A.D.* New York: Warner Books, 1976. Print.

8. Bradbury, Ray. American novelist, short story writer, essayist, playwright, screenwriter and poet, was born August 22, 1920 in Waukegan, Illinois.

9. Hsieh, Tony. *Delivering Happiness, A Path to Profits, Passion and Purpose.* New York: Hachette Book Group, 2010. Print.

10. Ford, Henry. He was an American industrialist and the founder of the Ford Motor Company. He invented the assembly line for automobile manufacturing, and designed the famous Model T. (July 30, 1863-April 7, 1947)

11. Shinn, George. *The Miracle of Motivation*. 2nd edition. Illinois: Living Books, 1994. Print.

12. Heath, Chip, and Dan Heath. *Switch: How to Change Things When Change Is Hard*. Canada: Random House, 2010. Print.

13. Faulkner, William. An American writer and Nobel prize laureate from Oxford, Mississippi.

Innovation

14. Govindarajan, Vijay—the Earl C. Daum 1924 Professor of International Business and the Founding Director of Tuck's Centre for Global Leadership Vijay is an expert on strategy and innovation. He was the first Professor in Residence and Chief Innovation Consultant at General Electric. BusinessWeek, The Economist, Forbes have cited him, and The London Times as the top thought leader in strategy.

15. Trimble, Chris—an expert on making innovation happen in large organisations. Chris Trimble has dedicated the past ten years to studying a single challenge that vexes even the best-managed corporations: how to execute an innovation initiative. His work came to fruition with the 2010 publication of *The Other Side of Innovation—Solving the Execution Challenge.* He has also published three lead articles in the *Harvard Business Review,* including "How GE is Disrupting Itself," in October 2009, with GE Chairman and CEO Jeff Immelt and Vijay Govindarajan. Chris is on the faculty at the Tuck School of Business at Dartmouth.

16. Govindarajan, Vijay and Chris Trimble. *The Other Side of Innovation: Solving the Execution Challenge.* Boston, MA: Harvard Business Review Press, 2010. Print.

17. http://www.vijaygovindarajan.com/2010/08/the_other_side_of_innovation_s.htm.

18. Tibolt, Frank. *A Touch of Greatness.* 2nd edition. San Dimas, CA: Mushtaq Pub., 1999. Print.

19. Govindarajan, Vijay. Trimble, Chris. *The Other Side of Innovation, Solving The Execution Challenge.* Boston, MA. Harvard Business Review Press. 2010. Print.

20. Toffler, Alvin. *Future Shock.* New York: Bantam Books. 1971. Print.

21. Godin, Seth. *Poke The Box.* New York: Do You Zoom Inc. 2011. Print.

Leadership

22. Gretsky, Wayne Douglas. Wayne Gretzky, nicknamed "The Great One," is widely considered the greatest hockey player of all-time.

23. Coughlin, Tomas Richard. An American football coach who is currently head coach for

the New York Giants of the National Football League (NFL).

24. Wakeman, Cy. *Reality-Based Leadership Ditch the Drama, Restore Sanity to the Workplace, & Turn Excuses Into Reality.* San Francisco, CA: Jossey-Bass. 2010. Print.

25. Conant, Douglas, and Mette Norgaard. TouchPoints, *Creating Powerful Leadership Connections in the Smallest of Moments.* San Francisco, CA:Jossey-Bass. 2011. Print.

26. Einstein, Albert. (14 March 1879-18 April 1955) He was a physicist who is widely regarded as one of the most influential scientists of all time. He is best-known for his Special and General Theories of Relativity, but contributed in other areas of physics. He won the Nobel Prize in physics for his explanation of the photoelectric effect.

27. Gerstner, Louis V Jr. *Who Says Elephants Can't Dance? Inside IBM's Historic Turnaround.* USA. Prentice Hall. 12 October 2004. Print.

28. Gibbon, Edward. *The History of the Decline and Fall of the Roman Empire.* B & R Samizdat Express. London. 2009. Print.

29. Welch, Jack. 29 *Leadership Secrets.* USA. McGraw-Hill. 2003. Print.

Conclusion

30. Glascow, Arnold. An American humorist. (1905-1998).
31. Luntz, Frank. *Win: The Key Principle to Take Your Business from Ordinary to Extraordinary.* New York: Hyperion. 2011. Print.

ABOUT THE AUTHOR

A regular keynote presenter at global industry conferences Paul Rigby also consults with business partners and frequently assists with partner company change, innovation and leadership efforts. Paul knows and understands business and what it takes to lead successful businesses in times of change and diversity. He has an incredible energy and passion and an ability to translate his hands on experience to the business world. He has learned from personal experience how to turn businesses around.

Paul conducts numerous speaking engagements in over 20 countries per year. He also serves as President, International Operations for International Thought Leader Network (ITLN); he is a certified master consultant for the Leading Innovation Workshop™ based upon the works of Vijay Govindarajan and

Chris Trimble from the Tuck School of Business at Dartmouth, Leading Bold Change™ based upon the works of Harvard Professor, John Kotter, Leading Change™, Leading Positive Performance™ based on the work of Shawn Achor CEO of Aspirant and a world leading expert on human potential and Learn To Lead™ a 5-day leadership program for emerging leaders.

Paul's proven ability to conduct business on a global stage gives him the experience to assist organisations of any size or scale to successfully reach their business objectives. Paul's easy going demeanour combined with years of practical line business experience make him a valued consultant partner to all of his clients.

Today, besides his public speaking engagements, Paul leads the international efforts of ITLN by facilitating client engagements, workshops, consulting and coaching ITLN business partners as well as overseeing its global distribution network on behalf of numerous best-selling authors.

Paul received his Bachelor of Commerce Degree at Rhodes University in Business Administration and Mercantile Law and later completed his Executive Development Program at Wits Business School.

Contact Paul at:

email: paul@paulrigby.biz

Web: www.paulrigby.biz